From My Heart to Yours

To DJ

Randall L Carpenter

Oct 2020

RANDALL CARPENTER

PAGE PUBLISHING, INC.
Conneaut Lake, PA

First originally published by Page Publishing 2020

ISBN 978-1-64628-847-2 (pbk)
ISBN 978-1-64628-848-9 (digital)

Printed in the United States of America

This book is dedicated to my four grandchildren, Weston Dunham, Tennley Belle Carpenter, Quinton Dunham, and Oliver William Carpenter. When you grow up, I hope the words in this book help you understand life and how important it is to love one another. I love all of you very much.

Contents

Foreword

Randy Carpenter's writings, like his life, are filled with grace and wisdom. Having served as one of his pastors for several years, I have come to realize that he was also pastoring me through his words of encouragement, his insightful writing, and his faithful presence and service.

He continues to write about life, love, and the many circumstances we face in our daily living. What else is there that so richly deserves our time and attention!

Randy's deep and authentic love for God, his family, his church, and the people he encounters is an inspiration to all who know him. And he doesn't just talk the talk (or write the words). His life is an incarnation of what you will read on these pages.

He's one of those people I describe to my wife as the real deal.

I am delighted that in this, his third book, he continues to offer the gifts of friendship and gentle guidance to those who know him—and to those who don't. You will be blessed and encouraged, and perhaps even come to know and understand yourself better as you move (slowly, I hope) through these pages.

Kenny Faught is an elder in the United Methodist Church and retired senior pastor from St. Mark United Methodist Church, Knoxville, Tennessee.

Introduction

From My Heart to Yours is a book of writings and inspirations that have helped form a bond between myself and my readers. It has allowed me to open my heart and give to my readers words of hope and moments of reflection. The relationships I have developed have been forged through honesty, humility, and commitment. In this age of technology, it has become possible to feel close to others yet be miles apart. It has allowed us to share our thoughts and feelings openly and create a strong sense of belonging with people we have never met. Though this technology is often abused and misused for personal reasons, when it is used to share love, concerns, and hopes of inspiration, it bridges the miles between people. I have tried for the last several years to share my thoughts and fulfill a promise I made to God after my open-heart surgery. This experience has added so much to my life. The relationships I have created, the friendships I have renewed, and the special bonds I have forged all mean so much to me. If you have ever read, liked, loved, or shared anything important in your life, this book will please you greatly. After you read *From My Heart to Yours*, our hearts will come to know each other very well. *From My Heart to Yours* is a book you will enjoy if your heart is open, your life is not perfect, and you still have hope for this world. My mission is not to educate you but inspire you to look beyond the surface of life and be motivated to never give up.

A Heart Never Knows

A HEART NEVER KNOWS appreciation
until someone with nothing
says thank you.

A HEART NEVER KNOWS beauty
until it looks past what the world
shuns and into someone's soul.

A HEART NEVER KNOWS compassion
until it's embraced by arms of love.

A HEART NEVER KNOWS
determination
until it learns to never give up.

A HEART NEVER KNOWS
encouragement
until someone makes it believe in itself.

A HEART NEVER KNOWS fear
until it's the only thing keeping
it from succeeding.

A HEART NEVER KNOWS greatness
until it sees it change the world.

A HEART NEVER KNOWS hope
until it realizes it's the thing
that allows us to dream.

A HEART NEVER KNOWS innocence
until it looks into the eyes
of a newborn child.

A HEART NEVER KNOWS joy
until it realizes everything
that makes it happy.

A HEART NEVER KNOWS kindness
until it hears words softly
spoken with a smile.

A HEART NEVER KNOWS loneliness
until it's alone in the darkness.

A HEART NEVER KNOWS mercy
until it sees it shown to someone
in their weakest moment.

A HEART NEVER KNOWS need
until it finds itself with nothing.

A HEART NEVER KNOWS
omnipotence
until it believes we never walk alone.

A HEART NEVER KNOWS peace
until it releases all malice
and learns to forgive.

A HEART NEVER KNOWS quietness
until it feels contentment in its life.

A HEART NEVER KNOWS respect
until it learns showing character
and integrity will lead you there.

A HEART NEVER KNOWS sacrifice
until it has willingly given up
something it can never replace.

A HEART NEVER KNOWS tenderness
until it has felt the gentle touch
of someone it loves.

A HEART NEVER KNOWS
understanding
until it meets someone who
has walked the same road.

A HEART NEVER KNOWS victory
until it realizes what you overcome is
greater than what you accomplish.

A HEART NEVER KNOWS wisdom
until it understands the advice
it receives possesses more than
an answer to its question.

A HEART NEVER KNOWS youth
until it's nearly gone, and it looks back
on everything it did or all it missed.

And lastly,

A HEART NEVER KNOWS
what life holds tomorrow
for those who love what they do
and share what they believe.

Inspired by Lauren and Leanna Price
The Price Sisters

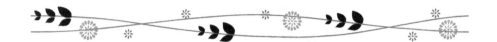

Every day, you are either adding to or taking away from your reputation. The consistency of your behavior is what builds your reputation. Depending on the reputation you have created, it either defends you against incrimination or makes you the prime suspect.

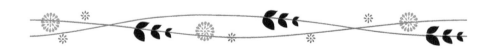

Most of the things that guide us happen
early in life. As we get older, those things
may become challenged or blurred.
Whether you change at that point or not,
be careful what controls your life doesn't
make you less loving, compassionate,
or forget where you came from.

Sometimes our dreams in life feel like the stars in the sky. They shine brightly in our mind but seem so far away. Don't fear the distance between you and your dreams because every dream touched in life begins and ends the same way, with a single step taken toward it each day.

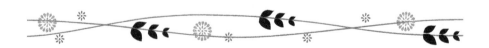

The image you project to others often leads to the amount of respect you receive. If you have respect for yourself in the way you look, act, and speak then, others will think more highly of you. Only when you are alone are you not projecting who you are to others.

To love others, you must first love yourself. Knowing what makes you happy gives you the knowledge of what to do for others. But more importantly, if you don't first love yourself, you will become dependent on others and their definition of love.

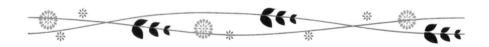

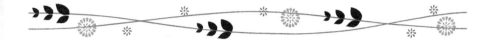

It's sometimes puzzling how some people will choose the most challenging way of doing things. This happens because people don't always do things the easiest way—they do them the way they feel the most confident. Try to be patient with the insecurities of others.

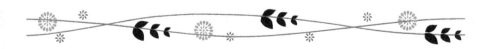

Don't allow the compromises of others to affect what you hold important in life. Unless you have principles in which you live by, you will eventually find yourself with no direction and very little to believe in.

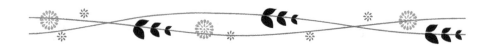

Sometimes what we think we need in life will be around the next corner. That may be the case, but if you go around enough corners, it will bring you back to where you started, and you realize it's where you belonged all along.

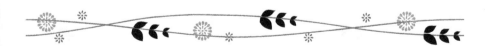

Getting mad about something just to
prove a point only creates more problems
that you'll have to apologize for later. It's
hard enough sometimes to explain why
you're mad, but just to prove a point
is impossible to justify to anyone.

What we fear most giving up in life may be the thing that is holding us back. The first sign of this happening is when it becomes an obsession instead of a choice in our life.

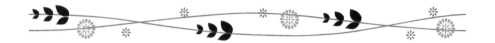

In life, we all have mountains we must climb. Some are higher than others, but it's not the height of the mountain you conquer but the satisfaction you feel in reaching the top and looking back at your journey along the way.

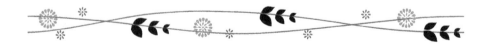

Though pride may be a reason not to do something, it should not be our excuse for denying we have a problem. Sometimes what we deny only adds more creditability to the fact we need help for something we can't see.

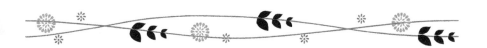

One of our greatest strengths of character is shown when we recognize our vulnerability and acknowledge we have a problem. Once we accept our mistakes in life, we can then begin changing them.

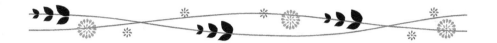

Some of our greatest surprises in life
begin with a smile and a hello. Someone
who may change your life forever
maybe just a smile and a hello away.

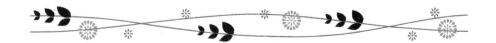

Sometimes a leap of faith only needs to be a single step forward as you go down to one knee to pray about something. Have faith in your faith, and let it help you make your decisions in life.

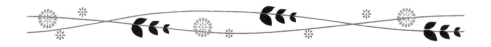

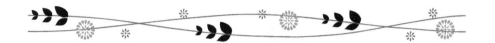

Life is about finding that spark that motivates you. It's seeking your purpose and pursuing it relentlessly. It may be a skill, a passion, or even a movement that drives you to leave your comfort zone and lead. Every day you want to be a little better than you were yesterday.

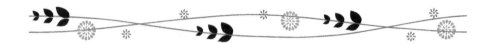

A content life is when you realize all
the things that you are grateful for far
exceed all the things you worry about.
Let the blessings in your life give
you strength as you deal with those
things that challenge your patience.

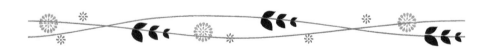

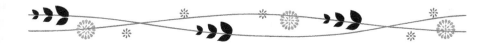

It would be so much nicer if the good things we've done in the past could be remembered as well as the mistakes we've made. Don't let your mistakes from the past determine your life in the future.

The greatest influence we have on
others are when they are moved to
be better, inspired to lead others, and
realize a greater purpose in themselves.
When someone sees something in
you that they want in themselves, you
have made a difference in your life.

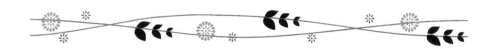

Some misunderstandings are not due to what someone said but what someone thought they heard. It's just as important for someone to listen closely as it is for someone to speak clearly.

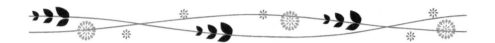

We've all been told to think before you speak. The downside of not doing so is realizing later what you said and not being able to apologize immediately for it. Don't hold your apology out of embarrassment. If you do so, it becomes heavier with every passing day.

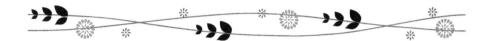

Never doubt what God can do for you. If He can change a caterpillar into a butterfly, He can change your life into something beautiful as well.

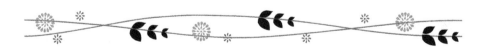

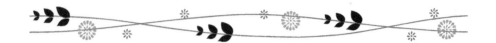

In life, what you say does more than explain yourself. It leaves an impression of you behind. People may forget what you say, but the impression you made on them may stay with them forever. Be kind, be considerate, and smile. A smile is a silent compliment you give to others.

Our greatest successes in life are not the things others praise us for. They are the things that quietly keep our life together and bring happiness to those around us. It takes great intelligence to invent something, but it takes a genius to keep everyone happy.

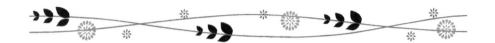

Sometimes the greatest things we do in life are things we have no idea we've done. Don't let this concern you. This means the way you're living your life is making a difference even when you're not trying to do so.

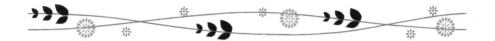

Few people in life reach the star they dreamed of touching. But in their attempt to do so, they touched the clouds and forget what an accomplishment that is in life. You're far more successful than you think, and you've accomplished many things you don't even realize.

Sometimes our greatest encouragement is the way some people handle the struggles in their life. Though they are deeply burdened, they remain grateful and hopeful. This happens when you count your blessings first and your burdens second. The first list is always much longer.

Faith is more than believing. It's also about living. It's taking what you believe and applying it to every part of your life. It's being an example, not of all-knowing, but of all loving, forgiving, and accepting. Faith is not only what you believe. It's what you live.

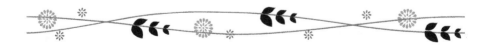

One of our greatest gifts to each other is consideration. When we are considerate of others, it creates trust, respect, and friendships. Though it rarely costs us much to be considerate, it can mean the world to someone who receives it.

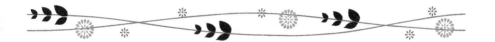

Loving someone in their time of need
is often more about what you do
than what you say. Just as a picture
paints a thousand words, so does
a loving embrace. Sometimes our
greatest love for someone is the one
that requires no words to express it.

Life is made up of thousands of events, encounters, and moments that alter our life every day. Everyone we meet in life changes us in some way. Though we may not remember everyone we meet, they still were part of our past that led us to who we are today.

People are different than they used to be. Today, people are like unfinished puzzles looking for a missing piece and finding it in something that offends them. The missing piece in people's lives is not what should offend them. It's what should inspire them.

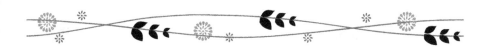

Have you ever noticed some things we say to ourselves always seem brilliant until we say them out loud? This is why we need good friends in our life, so we have someone to test our theories on before we embarrass ourselves in front of others.

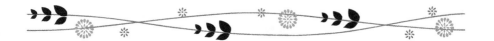

Sometimes in life, we feel like we spend more time apologizing than saying, "You're welcome." This is because society has made us more aware of not offending people. Don't live your life based on the opinions of others. Live it based on your opinion of yourself.

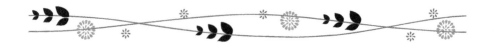

We live by God's grace every day. From each breath we take to the rhythmic heartbeat that silently keeps us alive, we live by God's grace. Cherish these gifts and be thankful because God's plan for you is not yet complete.

Words we say are remembered for a second or for an eternity in someone's heart. Our words must build others up, not tear them down. Make sure your words are encouraging, loving, and appreciative because words that insult, demean, and hurt are rarely forgotten.

The strength in any relationship is not how much you do for each other or how many loving words you say. It's found in the respect and consideration each has for the other that becomes as much a part of their relationship as loving gestures.

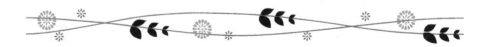

If our heart had eyes, we would see when we were making a mistake. If our heart had arms, we would be able to push some people out. But even if our heart did have these, it would still not change the fact love is blind and we hold on to those we love no matter what.

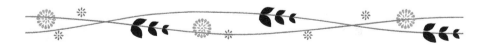

In life, we make many deals, compromises, and promises in order to do what we want to do. We rationalize our decision and convince ourselves it will be okay. Unfortunately, all this is done within us when we're deciding to do something we know we should not do.

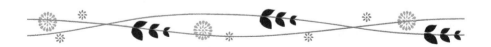

In life, it's sometimes better to be known for what we don't do than what we do. We often lead others more by the things they don't see us doing than the things we do. Displaying a strength of choice tells others we are confident in ourselves and strong in our convictions.

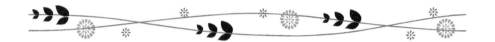

Sometimes it's not the things we did that haunt us. It's the things we didn't do. We had opportunities to show our compassion and grace but stood silent. We allowed a rudeness to go unchallenged and have regretted it ever since. These are things that often bother our heart forever.

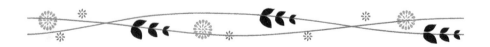

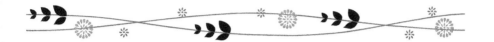

You don't have to be loveable before God
will love you. It makes no difference
what you've done, what you've said,
or how you've destroyed your life up
to now. God loves you even when
you don't think you're loveable.

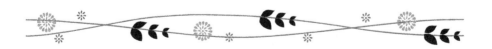

Sometimes we cannot avoid being sad.
But being happy or sad is often a choice.
We choose to see the beauty of the rose
petals or the sharpness of the thorns.
Don't be consumed by things that sadden
you and fail to see all the joy around
you. Never let this world steal your joy.

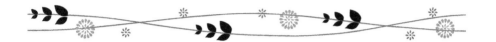

Sometimes the most wonderful moments
in our life are not the things we plan.
They are those moments that happen
suddenly that we never expect and
often leave the deepest memories.
Sometimes we should let our mind rest
and let our heart lead for a while.

My blessing for you today: Go with my prayers following you closely, God's love surrounding your fully, and a smile to light your path. Don't hide the goodness of your heart, and don't be afraid to lift others up with words of appreciation and gratitude.

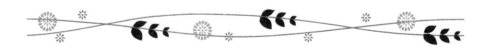

Sometimes the greatest weight we
lift in life is the burden we lift from
someone's shoulders through our words
of encouragement. Strengthened by
compassion, understanding, and mercy,
our words of hope may remove a burden
they have carried for a lifetime.

Inspired by and used with
permission from Natalie Fox

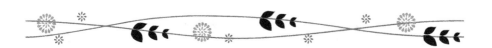

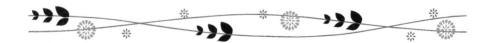

Some of our greatest expressions of love require no words or personal sacrifices. It costs nothing to show compassion, and a smile is a silent compliment you give to others.

If we could rewind time, we would bring back those we've lost and moments we cherish from our memories. We could correct mistakes and make amends where we know we were wrong. Sadly, we can't do this, but we can learn to never waste a moment in life and cherish those we love.

One of our greatest strengths in life is realizing what's not our problem. It's okay to help, but it's not necessary to inherit the problem.

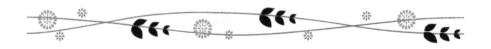

Sometimes life doesn't seem fair. We suffer losses, disappointments, and problems that never seem to go away. We seem to gain today and lose it tomorrow. Life is all about perspective. Don't look at what goes wrong, but what goes right. Your joys always outnumber your problems.

There are people in our life that no matter what we say, they always know our heart. These are the ones that believe in us most. There is nothing like old friends that never leave your heart.

Inspired by and used with permission from Diane Crowe LeGuillon

For some people, the truth is hidden
behind an unwillingness to accept it.
Most people who know you love you.
They have nothing but your best interest
in mind when they say things to you.
Don't let your pride or stubbornness
keep you from hearing the truth.

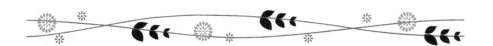

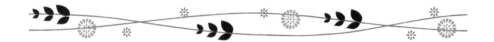

The collective efforts of many hearts help God place miracles in our life. One person says something that touches our heart, another helps reinforce our faith, and another shows us love we desperately need. All these acts of grace prepare us to see God's miracles in our life.

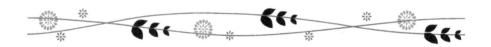

Though we cannot always choose what will control our lives, those things we surround ourselves with have an impact. If we surround ourselves with happiness and joy or hate and ugliness, one will be stored away and leak out into our life. We emulate what we most see in life.

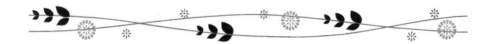

One of the greatest motivations a person can have is to know they are appreciated. When you're appreciated, your heart and mind are free to dream.

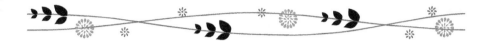

Negativity breeds positive thinking. People who are too negative make others positive they don't want to be around them. Don't let your negativity produce this positive feeling in those around you.

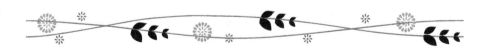

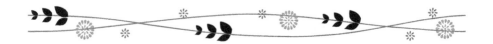

In life, it's not the physical touches that we remember the longest. It's the things that touch our heart. What touches our skin slowly fade away, but what touches our heart may live forever. Every embrace brings us joy, but those things that touch our heart often bring us love.

Some of our greatest rewards in life are not the wealth we accumulated or the positions we ascended to. They're the times we chose to love others unconditionally, to bring joy to their life, and to make memories that will keep them in our heart forever.

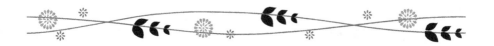

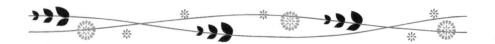

Like a drive down a sunny country road, life takes us through moments of sunshine and dark shadows. Like this road, we never know what may be around the next bend. Don't fear what life may have waiting for you. Rejoice in the sunshine today and deal with the rain tomorrow.

I believe there will be sunshine following the rain that falls upon me. I believe there will be calmness following the strongest winds in my life. And I believe I'm loved even when I feel unlovable. I know all this because I believe in the One that does it all.

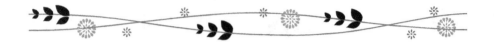

A smart person can tell you how something works. An intelligent person can tell you why it works. But an experienced person can tell you if it will work. When you're looking to get the best answer to what to do, go with the person who's doing the job now.

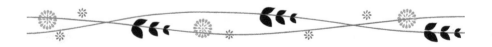

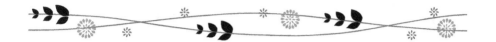

In life, every great success begins with a challenge. Don't be dissuaded by the difficulty of something or the amount of time it will take to accomplish it. Perseverance and determination are the two strong legs that every great success stands on.

A memory is the capturing of a moment in our life that touched our heart, changed our lives, or brought us closer to those we love. It's sometimes all we have left when all that's left is us.

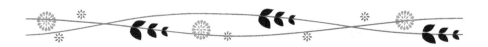

We all have clouds in our life. These clouds are the problems, annoyances, and nuisances that we have no controls over. It's easy to let these clouds hide the sunshine in our lives. Try to look through the clouds and enjoy the sunshine that shines above them.

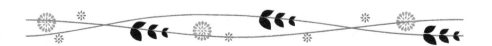

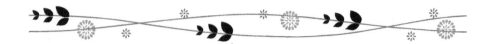

What if there was a mirror that reflected what's in your heart rather than an image in the mirror. We often try to hide things in our heart that others never know. Thinking about the reflection you'd see, would your heart be one of love or one of confusion?

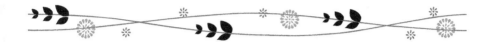

Every day you must carry with you
the tools to succeed. Those tools are
innovative thinking, a willingness to learn,
and a positive attitude. With these tools,
you are expanding your thinking and
absorbing as much knowledge as possible
while maintaining an optimistic outlook.

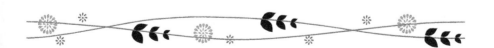

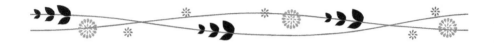

Seldom is our influence on others
more significant than how we react
to disappointment in our life.
Disappointment has a way of bringing
out the true nature of a person. How
we handle disappointment is seen
by others and leaves an impression
on them they do not forget.

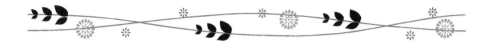

We all follow paths in life that lead us toward success or away from it. The insight we show in choosing a proven path increases our chances of success. Though no way is a guarantee, some roads are sure to lead us in the wrong direction.

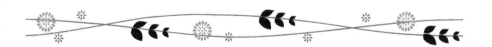

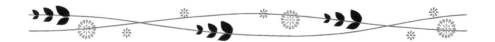

Acquiring experience in life is like the growth of a tree. We must endure some harsh winds, storms, and droughts in our life to keep growing. Every year we gain growth rings of experience that make us stronger and more resilient. Like the growth of a tree, experience takes time.

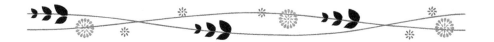

Sometimes in life, we build walls around ourselves to keep others out. It may be a wall of silence, a wall of bitterness, or a wall of guilt. No matter what your wall is made of, it isolates you. Be careful it's not a wall so high you cannot see those who love you.

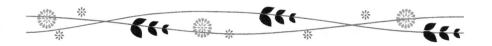

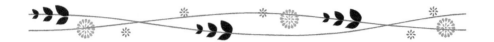

Don't let what you don't know convince you that you cannot learn what you have not tried. No one is versed in every subject, and knowledge is something obtained over time, not acquired at birth. Believe in yourself and what you seek to learn will slowly become a reality.

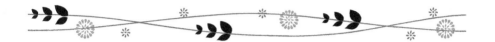

It's not easy to make something out of nothing, but you can't afford to make nothing out of something. You may not have everything you need in life, but what you have, you must find a way of making something from it. Life is one adapting moment after another.

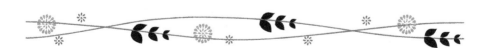

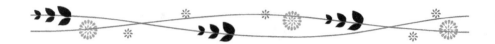

Every day we should open our eyes with the same hope for the day— to be in the right place, at the right time, to do the right thing. Life presents us with opportunities to do this every day. Look for them and make a difference in someone's life.

Sometimes the blessings in our lives
are hard to see. Some hide behind
our disappointments only to become
something we realize in the future was
a blessing. Trust all things happen for a
reason, and that reason may not be seen
until we live one of our tomorrows.

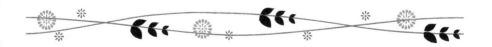

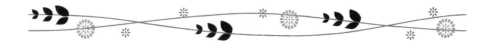

Those we truly love never leave us. They
move into our heart where they stay until
awakened by a memory to walk with us
again and hear all we still share together.

Sometimes we create our own weather within us. We feel calm, gentle breezes when we're happy. Something upsets us and the clouds begin to build. Our sunshine disappears, and we feel a storm building within us. This is when we must calm down before we rain down on others.

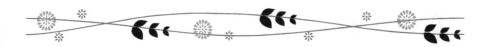

Memories are captured moments from
our past that abide in our heart until
we need them to teach us, guide us, or
remind us that we are never really alone.

In life, it's not always the things we don't know that concern us most. It's often the things we can plainly see, understand fully, but can do nothing about. Sometimes life is what we learn to accept, tolerate, or ignore. If we don't, we become captive to our every emotion.

Though we care, to some degree, what others think about us, it's more important to know how you feel about you. Is your life about living what you believe or one of constant compromise? Don't always follow the crowd. Sometimes you must stand alone as the parade passes you by.

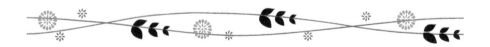

Sometimes in life, we need to work on our self-esteem before we can gain more self-confidence. It's difficult to gain confidence if you don't feel you deserve it.

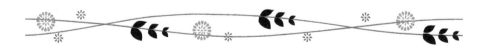

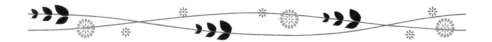

In life, our reputation is what speaks
for us when we're not around. It's what
others know about us and what defends
us from rumors and accusations. The way
we live our faith does the same thing.
If your faith is part of your reputation,
it speaks for more than yourself.

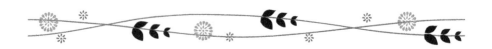

Our limitations in life are more about our expectations than our abilities. We never know what our limitations are until we test them with higher expectations. You're more significant than you think, stronger than you imagine, and every challenge you meet makes you more resilient.

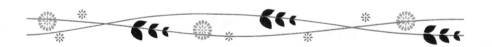

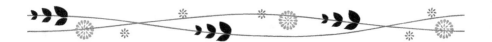

Sometimes we feel life chooses us instead of us choosing a life. We wonder why we go through all we go through. The answer to this may not be found in the life we live but in the loves we've treasured.

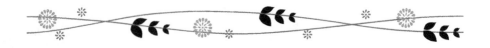

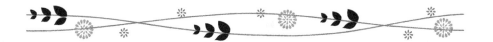

God is like our shadow. He's always with us. In our days of sunshine and happiness, we can see Him sharing the light with us. But even the happiest of lives have dark clouds and rain. Take comfort in knowing He is always there, standing beside us, even in our darkness.

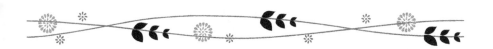

Those who take no chances in life succeed in rarely making mistakes. Sometimes it's better to try and fail than to do nothing and never know what you could have accomplished.

One of the best investments we make in life is the one we make in others. The potential for growth is excellent, and if done with love, there is a guarantee of high appreciation.

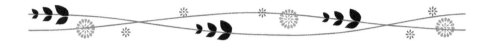

In life, we're the path that others follow or the road that leads them astray. We're the door that opens widely or the wall that keeps them out. How we treat people either show them the way or we're in their way. Your legacy in life is judged by the choices you make every day.

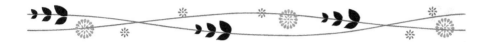

The surest way to become frustrated in life is to expect to change something that took years to create. This is especially true when it pertains to changes in ourselves. Don't let your enthusiasm for change overshadow your common sense. Take it slowly, and slowly you will change.

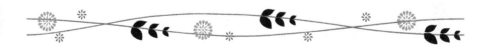

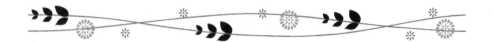

One of our goals in life should be to learn to say the most with the fewest words. Be secure in what you say, don't overexplain, and say enough to make others think for themselves. Sometimes the more we talk, the more we sound unsure of ourselves.

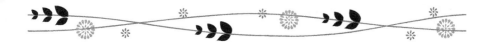

Life is filled with moments that are gone too quickly and those that seem to last forever. If we could hold on to those we want to continue and push out those that distress us, life would be perfect. But if life were perfect, Heaven would only be a place where we rested after life.

Some people think life is about what they know, what they think they know, and what they want to know. The problem with this is some people can't differentiate between what they know, what they don't know, and what is none of their business.

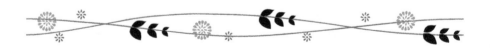

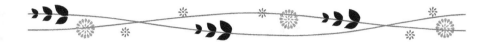

Sometimes our greatest satisfaction in life is not what we succeeded at but what we never gave up on. It's not what came easiest to us that we remember the longest. It's those things we had to work hardest for that stay with us forever.

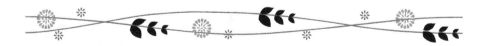

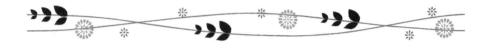

Our most significant lessons learned in life are often those that frustrated us the most, puzzled us completely, and required the longest time to master. They not only taught us many things, but they also gave us the confidence to never give up in life.

Life isn't about what we think we'll do, want to do, or might do. It's about what we actually do. Good intentions are like promises. Both have potential but mean nothing unless they are fulfilled. Great ideas should lead to great successes. Think, plan, and follow through.

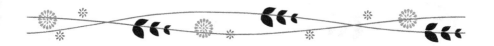

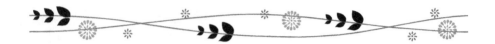

Sometimes the things we least expect in life mean more than the things we seek. The most joy we find in life comes from it finding us. A chance encounter that changed our lives, whom we fell in love with, and our greatest inspirations were all unplanned. It happens to us every day.

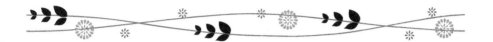

In life, we're never taller than when we stand up for what is right. We're never stronger than when we lift someone up who's down. And we'll never be richer than when we count our wealth by the number of people who love us. Life is not about what we gather but how much we give.

Getting angry in life is not a problem.
Staying angry is when it becomes
a problem. If you remain angry
too long, some of his crazy cousins
like spite, revenge, and hate show
up to cheer him on. Try to control
your anger before it becomes a
family reunion of crazy relatives.

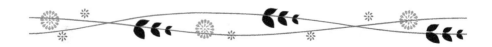

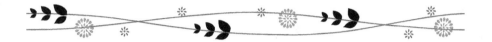

Today, whether it's your best day or your worst, it's a day you should cherish. Through your happiness and joy, you're uplifted by every moment. In your days of strife, you may feel overwhelmed, but you stand firm and face every challenge. Every day means something achieved.

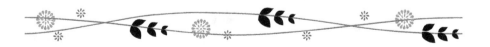

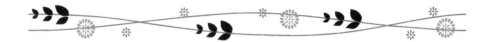

Not every step we take in life will be made with total assurance, be the same length, or be a step forward. Some may need to be backward to move forward. Don't feel you must always be moving forward in life. Sometimes a step backward gives you a better perspective.

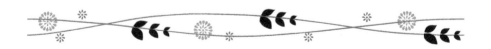

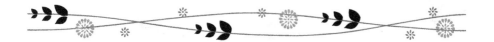

Some emotions we have are easy to see.
We don't hide happiness, sadness, or anger.
But some feelings we hide very easily,
like depression and loneliness. Sadly,
they're often hidden behind someone's
perceived happiness, sadness, or anger.
Be kind to everyone. It may help them.

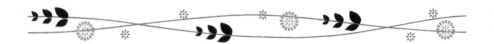

Life shouldn't be about your ability to fix problems. It should be more about your success in being able to prevent them from happening in the first place. Foresight is a more valuable characteristic than problem-solving.

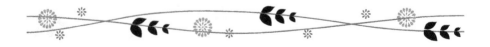

Self-esteem is not something you carry in your back pocket and take out every once in a while. It's something you use to help make decisions, shield you from manipulation, and give you strength to stand tall in life. Compromising your self-esteem should never be a choice.

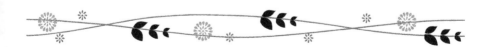

Sometimes our silence is not a sign
of anger, boredom, or depression.
It's not a way to shut others out, or
lack of anything to say. It's often
just our moments of reflection and
contemplation spent between us,
God, and the tranquility of silence.

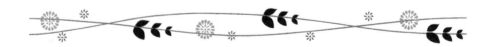

In life, people who draw conclusions from rumors, gossip, and misinformation are like an artist trying to paint a portrait with their eyes closed. When they rely on others to tell them what to paint, the person's likeness they finish may look nothing like the person they are.

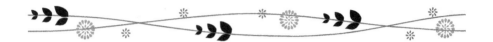

In life, we never stand taller than when we bend down to pick someone up. We never speak more clearly than when we defend someone who fears to speak. Our heart is never more open than we allow ourselves to forgive. What we do for others will be greatest examples in life.

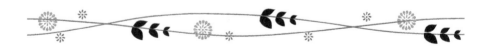

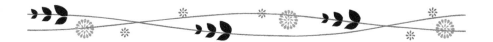

Little in life is ever accomplished by standing still. We fear change, but repeating the same behavior and expecting different results won't work. Believe in yourself, believe in your abilities, and move, because you're an easier target for others if you're standing still.

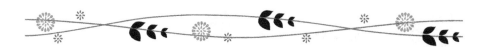

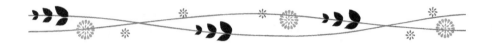

Making a difference in life doesn't require you change the world. It only requires you lead by example, learn from your mistakes, and share your compassion and love. If you succeed in doing these, you'll make a difference to those who mean the world to you.

Relying on the opinions of others to make decisions for you doesn't transfer the consequences of those decisions to them. They may take credit for good choices, but they will rarely accept the blame for bad ones. Don't be afraid to make your own decisions. We learn as we go.

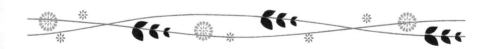

Not everything we do in life is going to be what others agree with. They will, sometimes not see the point, the purpose, or the need for what we do. That's okay, because life is not intended to be lived by committee approval but by the decisions we make and must live with.

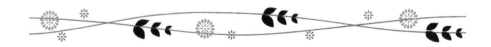

Our moments to show the kind of person we are become more apparent as we deal with the struggles in our life. The attitude we maintain in the face of our struggles tells others how much strength we possess. Often the things we overcome mean more to us than the successes we achieve.

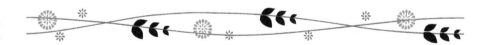

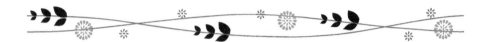

Sometimes what we look for in life doesn't seem to be what we already have. We think there's something better out there waiting for us. The problem with this is what we seek may not exist and what we risk losing may be precisely what we need but never realized.

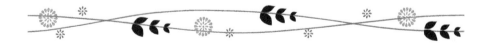

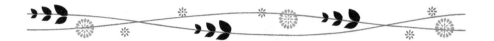

There are people in our lives that give us strength. They lift us up, hold us up, and pick us up when we fall. Their strength doesn't come from what they say or what they do. It comes from what they represent to us and our desire to not let them down.

Not everything you do today will make a difference today. Think about all the advice your parents gave you that you thought you ignored but now apply every day in your life. Sometimes the best advice takes a while to sink in.

Life should be about being inspired, finding things that make us happy, move our heart, or motivate us. To be inspired, we must be vulnerable to what's around us. When we begin to listen instead of talk, see instead of look, and feel instead of reject, inspiration soon follows.

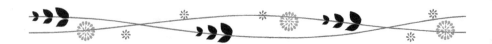

Sometimes we feel like our fears are greater than our faith. This doesn't mean we have lost our way; it means we're being tested by our emotions. Never lose faith in your faith. Trust what you already know in your heart. God will never abandon you.

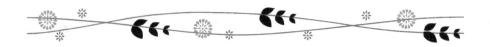

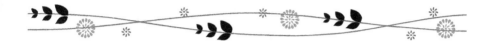

Every day we should have something in mind to accomplish. It may be something at work, a chore we've put off, or exercise we know we should do. The size of our accomplishment makes no difference because any achievement today could lead to changing our life tomorrow.

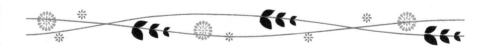

Sometimes having someone hurt our feelings can be our opportunity to learn the joy of forgiving. If everything we did in life were a success, we would never learn how humbling it is to fail. And if we made no mistakes, we would never know how gratifying a second chance can be.

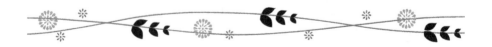

There's more to broken promises than someone's disappointment. Though someone can often give a reason why they broke their promise, it doesn't remove the fact someone was inconvenienced and made to feel unimportant. Fulfilling your promises shows your respect for others.

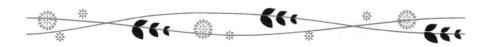

If every day you heard something positive about yourself, your self-esteem would improve. Likewise, if you heard something negative, it would suffer. This is why it's important to speak to people and smile because you never know which they last heard before you saw them.

Life is often not about what we're willing
to do but what we're willing to accept.
Sometimes we have no choice in what
we can do, but accepting a lesser effort
from ourselves can eventually become
a habit that's hard to break. Don't be
afraid to challenge yourself every day.

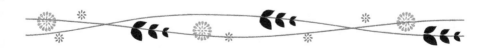

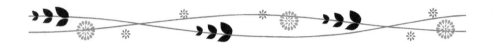

Sometimes we meet people and instantly see things within them we like. We see happiness in their smile, joy in their eyes, and confidence in their presence. But what we're seeing is often more than just them. Chances are, we're also seeing a love for God in their heart.

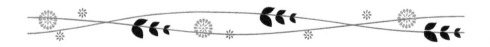

Don't allow the shortcomings of others
to lower your standards and compromise
what you spent a lifetime creating. In
life, establishing strong values is not
the hard part. It's maintaining them
in the face of all the challenges that
try to make you question them.

Live your life with confidence that you will succeed. All the years you have lived has given you abilities money can't buy, only years of experience can develop, and no one can take away. You are unique in countless ways and a model of resilience.

Sometimes we feel our life is destined for average with no moments of glory. This couldn't be further from the truth. Every day without you knowing it, your life influences those around you, touches someone's heart, or gives someone hope. There are no greater accomplishments.

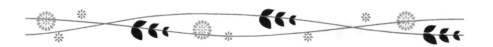

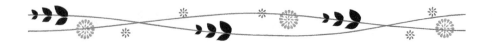

If our purpose in life is to make money, acquire glory, and receive great recognition, then some of us will succeed. But if it's meant to spread kindness, give hope to others, and lead by example, then fulfilling our purpose in life should never be out of our reach.

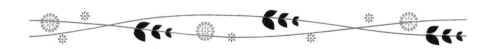

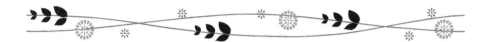

Many things in this world change and it's because they need to. But the need to care about one another isn't one of them. The world says trust no one and fear everyone. This isn't working very well. Maybe we need to go back to the days when we trusted everyone and feared no one.

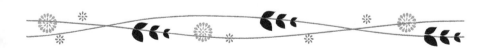

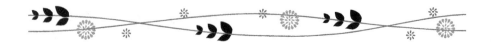

Building your life is a lot like building your house. Without a solid foundation, it's subject to the winds that blow, storms that rage, and shaky ground we all find ourselves on sometimes. Your foundation must be more than strong, though. It must be visible for all to see.

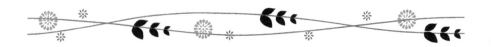

You never know the good you do until the good you've done changes someone's life. Then you realize all you've done was worth all you sacrificed to see this moment of happiness in someone's life.

The tears we shed in our life are not always tears of pain or sadness. They are sometimes the touch of God's hand upon our heart giving us comfort. Don't hide these tears out of fear they will be misunderstood because the grace they bring to us may live in our heart forever.

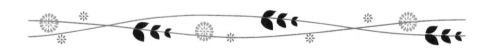

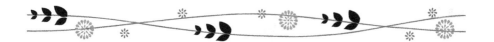

Life is sometimes about learning to bend but not break. Learning to compromise without sacrificing yourself. It's necessary to be steadfast at times, but realizing what you may gain later by compromising today is essential. Sometimes losing a battle leads to winning the war.

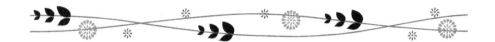

One of the things we must fight always is a feeling of apathy. The only thing worse than not doing something about an injustice we see is to not care about the injustice we see. When we quit caring is when we lose our ability to choose the person we are in life.

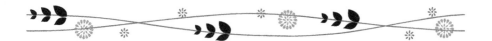

In life, some of our simplest gestures mean the most to other people. We never know the struggles others deal with. This is why it's important to speak to people, compliment others, and smile. Our gestures of kindness may be what someone needs to feel they are not invisible.

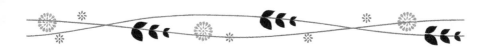

There will never be a point in our life where we know more than we don't know. It's been said everyone lacks intelligence, just on different topics. So when someone has an opinion about something they know nothing about, it removes all doubt which topics are theirs.

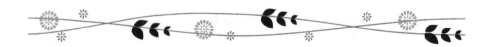

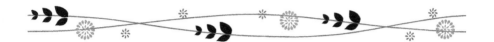

We all have giants in our lives who look out for us. They may be shorter than us, but we look up to them. These giants teach us much, protect us always, and often give us the strength to carry on. Who are your giants in life? Who do you look up to who has never looked down on you?

In life, what makes one person do good things and another not? What must happen to change a heart from love to apathy or hate? We may never know, but we know what can change a heart from anything to love. Share your faith because no heart is beyond God's ability to change it.

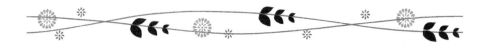

People who live their life always worrying
about what might happen will either
miss the joys of the present or fail to
recognize the potential of the future.
This is why we need to prepare ourselves
today to make what might happen
in the future something positive.

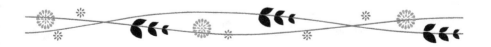

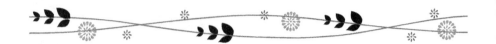

Sometimes in life, we fail to remember who we are and what we represent. We are more than ourselves. We are our family, our reputation, and part of a legacy formed by past generations. Never forget where you came from and those who will always be a part of you.

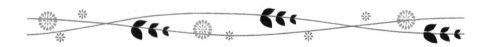

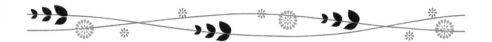

The gifts we give away freely are the greatest gifts we possess. They cost nothing but can often leave the greatest impression. A smile, a wave, or a nod of recognition pierces the imaginary wall that surrounds those we've never met. Be the first to respond and make someone's day.

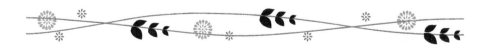

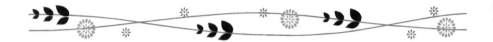

Sometimes we feel we're good enough to get by but not great enough to be a star. We think we know enough to communicate but not enough to be an authority. You're far greater than you think and know more than you realize because respect earned from a job well done is greatness.

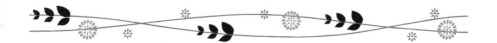

Most have heard of the power of
the pen and the sharpness of the
tongue, but sometimes the deafness
of silence is more damaging. When
you refuse to communicate with
someone, it creates uncertainty in
their heart. When you test someone's
love, you test their commitment.

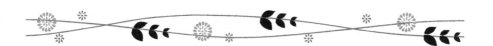

There are moments in our life that we never forget. They taught us something, touched our heart, or almost destroyed us. As tough as some of these moments may have been, they gave us perspective that we've never forgotten and use every day. Our memories of them keep us focused.

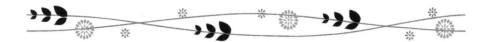

Often, the strength we rely on to oppose certain changes in this world comes from our faith. Our beliefs won't allow us to accept what we see happening around us. Unless we stand up for something, no one knows where we stand.

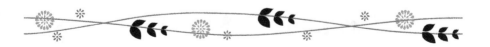

Resisting the temptations of this world can be difficult. Our ability to withstand them must be greater than the temptations we face. If we have faith in ourselves and confidence in our beliefs, the temptations we face will often be overcome by our common sense.

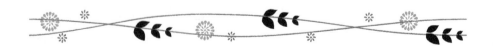

Most of our memories are like a beautiful quilt sewn together with a single thread of love, some pieces double-stitched to ensure they never come apart and others sewed with a strand of love only we can see. Cherish your quilt because memories are often our greatest comforter.

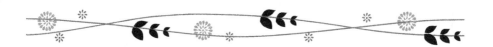

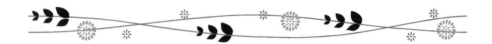

In life, the things we least expect are often the things we're forced to deal with. It's not always the well-made plans that demand our attention but the things we never see coming. Don't let this hold you back. It's in these moments of opportunity you may shine your brightest.

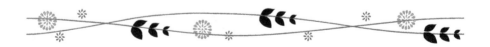

Sometimes in life, we have a second chance at love, friendship, or forgiveness. Though we have cried many tears from within, our hope of reconciliation has never left our heart. Never give up on hope because where there's hope, there's always a chance of a miracle.

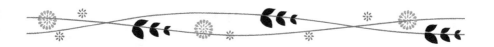

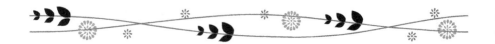

Change happens many times in our lives.
It occurs as we grow, as we learn, and
as we experience life. It's the changes in
our life that develop who we'll become.
But our most significant changes are
those we make in others through the
positive influences they see in us.

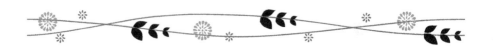

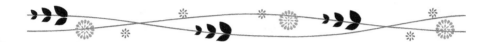

Some people dispute God exists. They cannot see Him, explain Him, or understand Him, so they ignore Him. This is what having faith is about. Believing in something that you sometimes cannot see, explain, or understand. It's about accepting a love you don't have to understand.

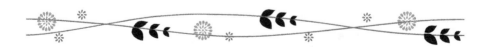

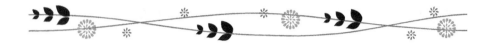

The beauty of life is not always in the images we see or the music we hear. It's also in the relationships we develop. Friendships that seem meant to exist and love that cannot be explained by mere words make life worth living. This is the beauty of life only our hearts can see.

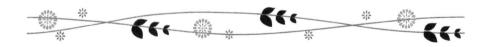

Sometimes it's easier to get offended than to try to understand why something happened. Behind everything that happens to us, there is an untold story and a series of events leading up to it. Try to be more understanding because we all have our own untold stories we deal with.

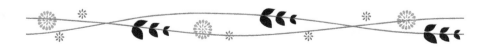

Those we count on in life are sometimes the ones we take for granted. It may be because they rarely fail us or because we get used to them and fail to appreciate them. Look at your life and take a minute to say thank you to those who make your life easier.

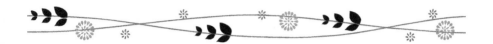

In life, it's not how well we plan, prepare, or perform but how it's interpreted by others. It's not always what we do but how we do it. Sometimes a softer voice is understood better than a loud explanation. We don't have to change our message, just our way of delivering it.

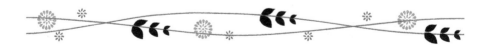

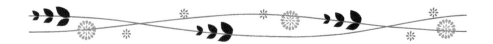

The significance of our walk-in life is not measured by the number of footprints we make but by the direction in which they are leading. We must understand others may follow and place their feet in our tracks. Are your footprints leading them toward or away from God?

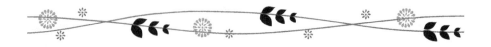

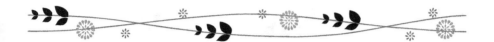

At times we feel like we're always apologizing for something or wish we had done something we didn't do. This isn't always caused by guilt but by our caring for others. Often what we think may have offended someone, they never noticed. Try to be less judgmental of yourself.

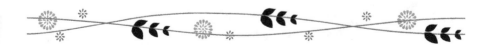

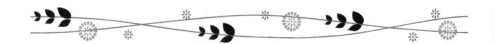

In life, if we expect ourselves to be perfect, we'll surely be disappointed. If making mistakes dissuade us from continuing to try, we will never succeed. Our greatest teacher will always be our mistakes. It's not what we fail at that's important. It's what we learn from it.

Four of the most significant words of hope in life are *love, motivation, encouragement*, and *inspiration*. From the love we receive from others, we're motivated to show encouragement to those around us and inspire them to never lose hope. It all begins with love.

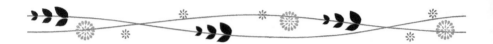

Two of our greatest motivators in life should be success and failure. Success because we seek to repeat what we previously accomplished, and failure to prove we don't give up. In life, there's a fine line between success and failure, and that line is usually perseverance and preparation.

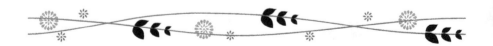

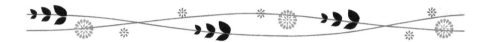

Being motivated by our successes is easier than being motivated by our failures. If we look at our failures as only a learning experience and not as a reflection of our ability, then receiving motivation from the experience becomes easier. Don't give up on your dreams. They may only be one attempt away.

Life is filled with many unspoken words. Words of love we've never expressed or words of apology we need to say. Don't be afraid to open your heart because sometimes it's what we finally profess from deep within that gives us our greatest relief.

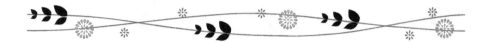

Sometimes in life, how we react leaves a greater impression than how we act. It may take us a lifetime to create a reputation others remember. But how we react to disappointment will be recalled instantly. Disappointment is frustrating, but don't take it out on those around you.

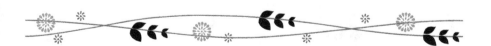

At times, we feel frustrated, confused, and exhausted. But even worse, we feel alone and unloved. Though we must endure a lot in life, we should never feel we're alone and unloved. God loves us through all we encounter. He is always listening when we need to talk.

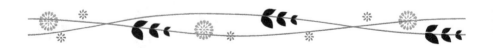

Try to love as deeply as you would want to be loved. Be as compassionate as you would hope someone would be if you were the one needing the help. And always show respect to others because their appearance is only half the story most people have lived.

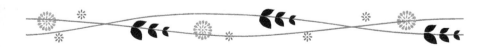

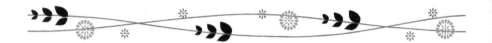

The longer our explanation of something, the better the chance of confusion, misunderstanding, and sounding like we're defending ourselves. Try to say what needs to be said without sounding like you're trying to convince yourself at the same time.

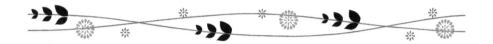

Life would be easier if it were like our computer. We could set the autocorrect and never make a mistake, delete what want to forget, and save what we want to remember. The problem is, we use everything in life to learn from and deleting anything may cause us to make more errors.

In life, there are no ordinary days. Our days aren't only what we need to do but what we may experience. We have many opportunities to learn, teach, or grow every day. Inspiration is more than a single moment experienced. It's taking the time to see what surrounds you every day.

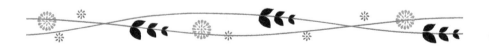

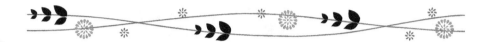

Sadness in our life creates cracks on our heart that sometimes never heal. But when we least expect it, someone's love touches our heart and renews our happiness. Love has always been the greatest healer. When it's given unconditionally, it can ease someone's deepest sorrow.

Inspired by and used with permission of Marie Cole Anderson.

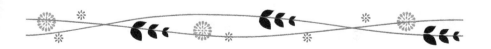

Sometimes in life, we don't need help. All we need to know is we're not alone. Knowing someone cares about us gives us strength. Don't assume those you care about know you care because you may be their strength and never realized it.

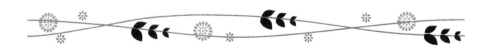

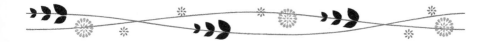

Your reputation in life is developed in two ways. First by what you choose to do and second by what you choose not to do. Once that is established, it becomes a question of consistency.

In life, we show love in many ways. One is when we must do something we dislike, but we do it anyway because it will make someone we love happy. We do this because our love for that person is greater than our dislike for what we have to do.

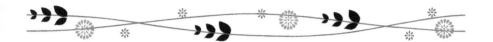

In our life, we've had people who made tender moments last forever. Their love lifted us up and filled our heart with hope. They became cornerstones of our memories. Sadly, some may no longer be with us, but because they taught us how to love, they will always be a part of us.

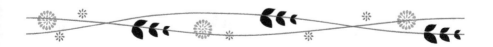

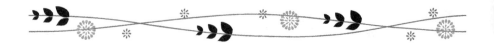

Height makes no difference when it comes to those we look up to in life. We may be taller, but we can still look up to someone. People who make a difference in us earn our respect because those we look up to never look down on others.

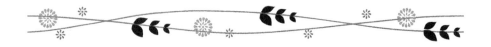

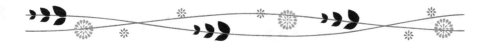

Dreams in our life must touch the clouds but also have feet that touch the ground. What lies between our dreams and the ground is reality. Reality is seeing the sacrifices needed, the long journey ahead, and the resolve required. Accepting these realities leads to our dreams.

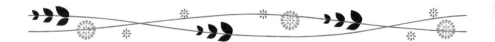

One of our greatest investments will be in our family. The appreciation in this investment often grows every day. You'll find the more you put into it, the higher the return. And the value of this investment increases as the interest in it grows with every passing year.

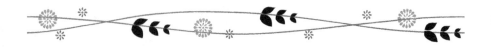

In life, there are three types of people: a wall, a window, or a door. Those who are walls stand in our way. Those who are windows, we see right through them. But those who are a door open themselves widely and embrace us, giving us the happiness we seek in life.

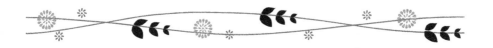

Sometimes in life, it's not what we say but what we don't say that says the most. When someone tries to solicit a negative response from you but you remain silent, it says a lot. Talking can be like fishing. Once you cast your line out, it's too late to regret where it landed.

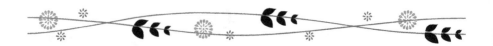

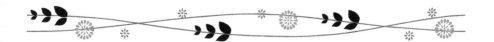

Making the right decisions in life is hard. We sometimes fear criticism. We need to remember those who choose to criticize often have the benefit of hindsight. You can only do the best you can with what you have under the circumstances at the time. Decide what feels right to you.

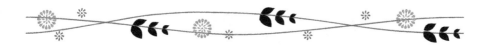

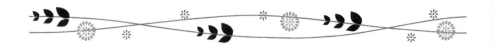

Making a difference in this world doesn't require you change the world. It requires you don't allow this world to change you by becoming apathetic. Once you begin to quit caring about what affects you in life, you start to change yourself more than the world around you.

In life, our emotions show themselves every day. We go from happy to sad to angry to remorseful all in one situation. Life is filled with moments that challenge us. The ones that bring out our darkest emotions we must learn to control. If not, they will take over our lives.

Brake lights we see as we drive are like problems in our life. If we see them early enough, we can avoid the crash. Though not always the case, there are often warning signs that alert us to future problems. Pay attention, and you may prevent a potential wreck in your life.

We all seek a calmness in our heart.
We want a peace that fills us with hope
and love. We desire the tranquility of a
content life and a joy we can embrace
every day. All this comes with knowing
you are unconditionally loved, and
you find this in the love of God.

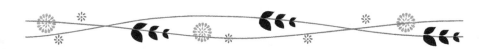

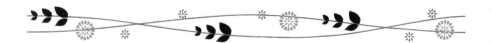

Sometimes our greatest influence on others is not in our words or even our actions. It's often in our decisions that affect others. How much we consider the feelings of others tells a lot about us. How kind, considerate, and empathetic we are leave an impression on others.

Sometimes in life, it's not the shortest route we take that gets us to where we need to be but the longest one. Often the journey is as important as the destination. You may be on that journey now. Be patient. There may be something that you're needing to learn along the way.

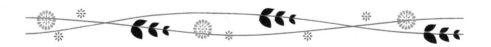

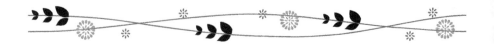

In life, it's not the number of days we live that means the most. It's the number of days we didn't sacrifice to anger, jealousy, or envy. It's about living every day to its fullest without regret. Love and joy make a happier life than spite and revenge.

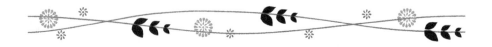

In life, it's not the battles we win but the ones we have the courage to fight. We may face unthinkable odds of prevailing, but nonetheless we take on the battle. Not every war will be won, but every conflict will prove we cared.

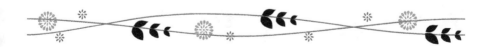

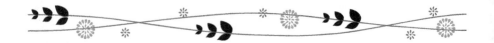

In life, we rarely care about anything we don't believe in. If we have no confidence in it, belief in it, or see any worth to it, it's difficult to know the importance of it. Sadly, this is how some people feel about themselves. We never know who needs to be lifted up every day.

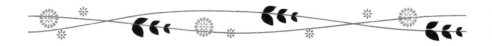

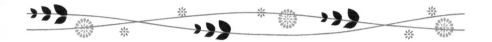

Sometimes the only things that separate those who do things and those who don't are the confidence to try and the courage to risk failing. Not everything we attempt in life will work, but those things we never try have no potential of succeeding.

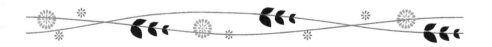

Sometimes in life, we don't know
what to do, so we must rely on what
we can do. Not every decision will be
correct, and others may be criticized,
but sometimes all we have in life is
our experience, wisdom, and common
sense to make our hardest decisions.

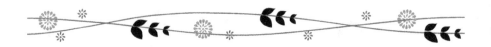

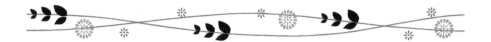

The greatest strength we possess is the one that lives within us that picks us up, props us up, and pushes us forward. It's the strength that assures us we are not alone and never without hope. It shows us through our faith we can endure all things.

One of our goals in life should be to prove who we are every day. We do so through our choices, the strength of our convictions, and our consistency. How consist ent we are in what we stand for tells others who we are.

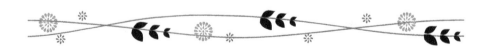

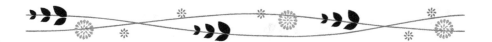

In life, most success is the result of great sacrifices that were made. Often those sacrifices were not made by us. Sometimes love requires giving up something so someone we love can succeed. Don't forget those who sacrificed for you. It was a gesture of love.

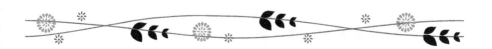

In life, you can't walk forward if you keep looking behind you. If you try, you will miss what is ahead of you, walk past opportunities you never see, and allow what you cannot change to affect what you can. Live for today and tomorrow, not to make up for yesterday.

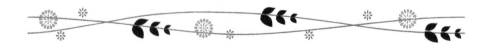

From our greatest disappointments can
come our most significant changes.
What may knock us down may also
open our eyes and allow us to see
changes we need to make. Whether
the changes will be something positive
or not depends on the perspective
we have when we stand back up.

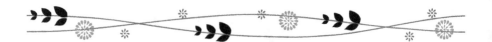

Every day we should try to be a little better than we were yesterday. Sometimes this requires we step back a step, regain our perspective, and then move two steps forward. Our greatest achievement isn't always where we end up but what we learn about ourselves along the way.

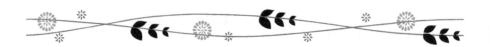

Sometimes there are limits to what we can do, what others can do, or what more can be done. Our mind doesn't want to accept this, but our heart knows it's true. When you face these moments, don't give up or give in. Instead look up and let God help you find your strength within.

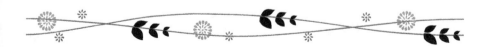

In life, we sometimes wonder if our chances to help change this world diminish over time. Actually it increases instead of decreases due to the experience we gain with age. Experience is acquired over time, and when we share it with others, it can change someone's world.

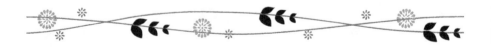

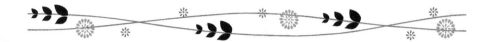

In life, we can't allow regrets to be something we dwell on. Allowing regrets to question if we would be happier had we followed another path is futile. Everything in life is a learning experience, and there are no assurances life would be better had we done it any differently.

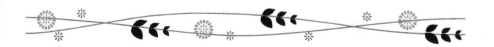

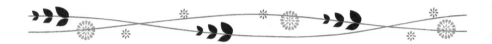

Sometimes miracles in life are not easy to see. They are hidden within things that went smoothly or in something tragic that could have been worse. Don't expect your miracles to be something miraculous. They are often quiet as a falling snowflake and subtle as a gentle breeze.

In life, we all hear voices. Some that have given us good advice and others out of love. But the one voice we all hear and have in common is our own. It's there to make us stop and think before we act. Don't ignore the voice within you. It speaks from years of experience.

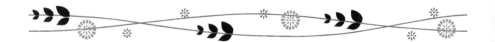

Everyone in life is a survivor. We've all been through things that may not have been life-threatening, but they were life changing. We should keep this in mind as we interact with one another. No one is without scars from the personal battles they have fought in life.

About the Author

Randall Carpenter has been writing since he was a young teenager. He has written over two thousand separate writings, and most are on deposit in the Library of Congress. Randall writes a daily inspirational writing on Facebook under the name Randy Carpenter and on Twitter under @rancathwritings. He holds a bachelor's degree from the University of Tennessee in Knoxville, Tennessee. He became a Stephen minister several years ago, and his insights have helped many people better understand themselves and the world around them. He held the senior lay leader position in one of the largest Methodist churches in the United States for many years. His words, observations, and insights will open your heart to the love of God.